The Ultimate Self-Teaching Method! **Level 2** REVISED EDITION

Play Piano Today!

A Complete Guide to the Basics

Speed • Pitch • Balance • Loop

To access audio visit:
www.halleonard.com/mylibrary

Enter Code
7451-7662-5850-8837

ISBN 978-1-5400-5948-2

7777 W. BLUEMOUND RD. P.O. BOX 13819 MILWAUKEE, WI 53213

Visit Hal Leonard Online at
www.halleonard.com

Contact us:
Hal Leonard
7777 West Bluemound Road
Milwaukee, WI 53213
Email: info@halleonard.com

In Europe, contact:
Hal Leonard Europe Limited
42 Wigmore Street
Marylebone, London, W1U 2RN
Email: info@halleonardeurope.com

In Australia, contact:
Hal Leonard Australia Pty. Ltd.
4 Lentara Court
Cheltenham, Victoria, 3192 Australia
Email: info@halleonard.com.au

Introduction

Welcome to *Play Piano Today! Book 2 Revised Edition*, the series designed to teach you the basics of playing the piano. If you've completed *Play Piano Today! Book 1 Revised Edition*, congratulations! Keep Book 1 handy for review and reference. Book 2 begins with the left hand on bass clef. Focusing on the left hand will strengthen your keyboard technique and reading skills, adding to the tools you need to play the piano with confidence and ease. Let's get started!

About the Audio

The accompanying audio will make learning more enjoyable as you progress step by step through each lesson at your own pace. Much like a traditional lesson, the best way to learn this material is to read and practice a while on your own, using the audio as a reference. If you'd like to play along with the demo track, use the Playback+ feature online to adjust the tempo as you learn each song. Every music track has been given a track number, so when you want to practice a song again, you can find it right away.

Contents

Music Review

In *Play Piano Today! Book 1 Revised Edition* we learned the basics of reading music on the treble clef. Let's review treble clef before we shift our focus to the bass clef.

Note Values

Music is written with symbols called **notes**. Each type of note has a specific rhythmic value. When the quarter note gets one beat, all other rhythmic values are determined by the quarter note.

quarter note = 1 beat

half note = 2 beats

dotted half note = 3 beats

whole note = 4 beats

Staff

Notes are placed on a **staff**, five horizontal lines and four spaces. Placement of these notes on the staff determines pitch, how high or low the note will sound. The higher the note is placed on the staff, the higher it will sound; the lower the note is placed on the staff, the lower it will sound. Since not all notes will fit on just five lines and four spaces, **ledger lines** are used to extend the staff.

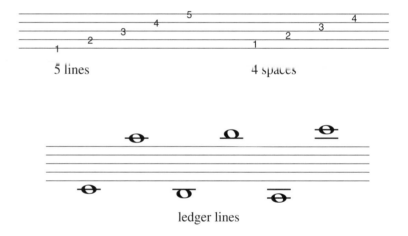

5 lines   4 spaces

ledger lines

Clef

A symbol called a **clef** indicates where the notes will be played on the keyboard. The right hand, which we focused on in Book 1, plays notes written in the **treble** clef. Let's review the names of the treble clef notes.

E   G   B   D   F
(Every Good Boy Does Fine)

F   A   C   E
(FACE)

Rhythm

To organize the notes on the staff into **measures**, **bar lines** are used. A **time signature** determines how many beats will be in each measure. The top number of the time signature indicates the number of beats per measure, and the bottom number names the note that gets one beat.

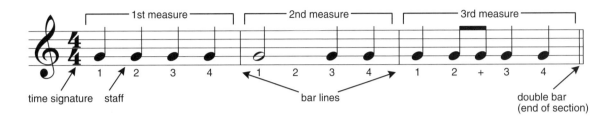

Intervals

Notes move along the staff in patterns of steps, skips, and larger intervals. Repeated notes stay on the same line or space; larger intervals skip one or more lines and spaces. Study the intervals written on the staff below.

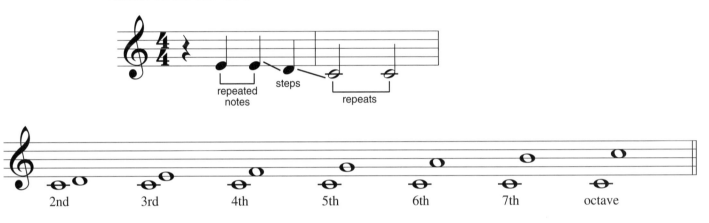

Treble Clef Sight Reading Review

Play this tune in treble clef with your right hand, looking for steps, skips, and larger intervals.

Simple Waltz

Track 1

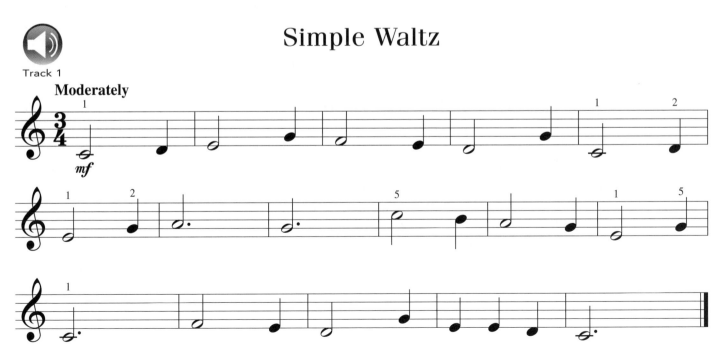

5

Bass Clef

The focus in *Play Piano Today! Book 1 Revised Edition* was on reading the treble clef and playing melody with the right hand. To be a well-rounded keyboard player it's important to be able to read the bass clef, and to have equal strength and dexterity in both hands.

The Bass Clef

As you know, the clef sign determines the pitches written on the staff. The **bass staff** looks like this:

The fourth line, which falls between the two dots of the clef sign, is designated as the pitch F; the first F below middle C. Because it designates the pitch F, this clef can also be called the **F clef**. Take a few moments to study the pitches written on the bass staff. Note that the names of the lines and spaces written in bass clef are NOT the same as the treble clef!

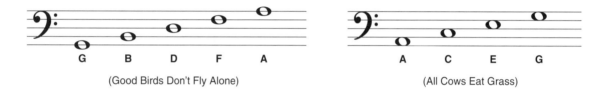

G   B   D   F   A   A   C   E   G

(Good Birds Don't Fly Alone)   (All Cows Eat Grass)

Bass Clef Note-Reading Practice

Scan the line of bass clef notes below. Set a timer. How quickly can you name the notes? Set the timer again. How quickly can you name, and then play the notes?

C Position for Left Hand

Five consecutive notes in a row, played by five consecutive fingers, is sometimes referred to as a "five-finger position," acting as a home base of sorts for simple tunes. Study the notes in C position below, written on the bass staff.

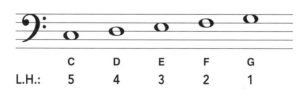

	C	D	E	F	G
L.H.:	5	4	3	2	1

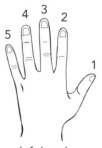

left hand

The popular Christmas tune "Jingle Bells" uses the five notes in C position. Once you've learned this securely with left hand, try adding right hand an octave higher. Playing the same part with both hands is called playing in **unison**.

Jingle Bells

Track 2

Words and Music by J. Pierpont

You're ready to play Beethoven's famous theme "Ode to Joy" from Symphony No. 9. Place left hand finger 5 on the C below middle C, with consecutive fingers on the notes that follow. Notice whether the notes repeat, move up by step, or down by step.

Ode to Joy
(Theme from Symphony No. 9)

Track 3

By Ludwig van Beethoven

Left Hand as Equal Partner

Even though right hand plays the melody much of the time in music written for piano, the left hand plays a far more important role than mere support. Accompaniments such as chords, arpeggios, and rhythmic patterns require a strong technique and comfort in moving around the keyboard.

Left Hand Warm-ups

Use the C position to play the following exercise. Play slowly at first, and as you feel comfortable, increase the tempo.

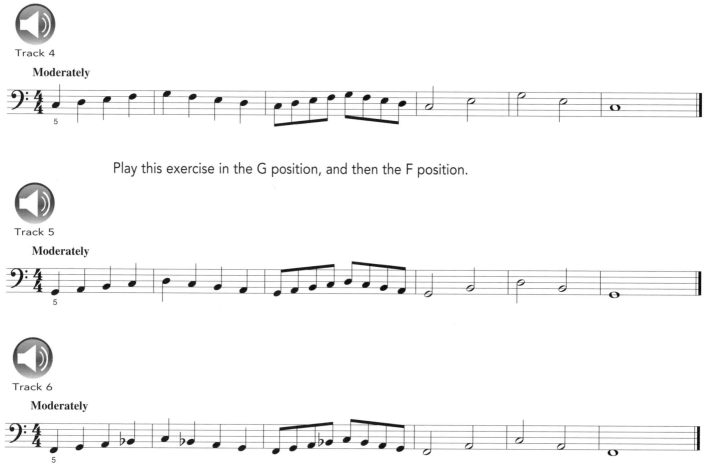

Track 4

Moderately

Play this exercise in the G position, and then the F position.

Track 5

Moderately

Track 6

Moderately

Left Hand Chords on the Bass Staff

In *Play Piano Today! Book 1 Revised Edition*, chords were notated using chord labels above the treble staff. Chords can also be notated on the bass staff. Here's an example of chords written on the bass staff. As you play the chords, listen for all the notes of the chord to sound at the same time. Pick your hand up as needed to move to each chord.

Track 7

Track 8

The chords you just played could be called **blocked chords**, as all the notes are played together, in a block. When written this way they even look a bit like a block, with all the notes stacked up on the staff. **Broken chords** are the opposite. Instead of playing the notes all together, they're played one note at a time. Broken chords are also called **arpeggios**.

Rhythmic Riffs and Accompaniments

Sometimes the left hand really gets to shine! Whether taking a turn at the melody, or playing a fun groove, the left hand can add a lot of style.

Jazzy Walking Bass

Track 9

Cool R&B

Track 10

Classic Rock Bass

Track 11

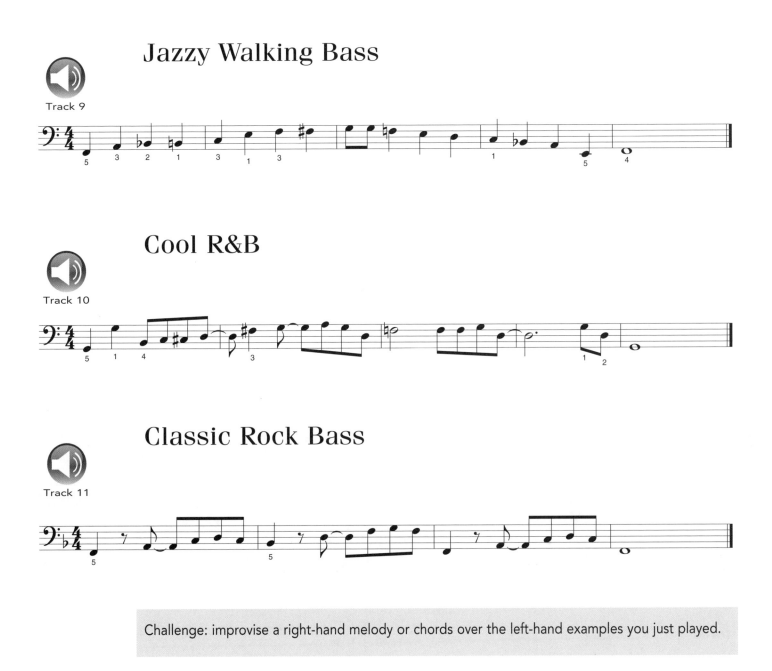

Challenge: improvise a right-hand melody or chords over the left-hand examples you just played.

The Grand Staff

Most piano music is written on the **grand staff**. The grand staff is made up of the treble staff and the bass staff connected with a bracket. When reading the grand staff, the right hand plays the treble staff and the left hand plays the bass staff.

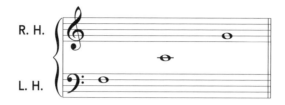

Playing on the Grand Staff

Play "Ode to Joy" notated on the Grand Staff. Notice that the melody moves from treble staff (right hand) to bass staff (left hand).

Ode to Joy

Track 12

By Ludwig van Beethoven

Set a steady quarter note beat before you play "Alouette," so the eighth notes are right in time. Remember, two eighth notes are equal to one quarter note.

Alouette

Traditional

Tempo and Dynamics Review

Find the tempo indication at the beginning of the song, right above the time signature. Look for dynamics and other expression marks in the music throughout. See the box below for a quick review.

	Dynamics and Expression	
p	piano	soft
f	forte	loud
mp	mezzo piano	moderately soft
mf	mezzo forte	moderately loud
rit.	ritardando	slowing down
a tempo		return to original tempo
	Crescendo (cresc.)	gradually get louder
	Decresendo (decresc.)	gradually get softer
	Slur	play smoothly; connected
	Staccato	play detached

Playing Hands Together

"Yankee Doodle" begins with left hand playing melody. In measure 9, melody switches to right hand, and the left hand harmonizes with C and G, ending with both hands playing melody together in the last two measures.

Yankee Doodle

Track 14

Traditional

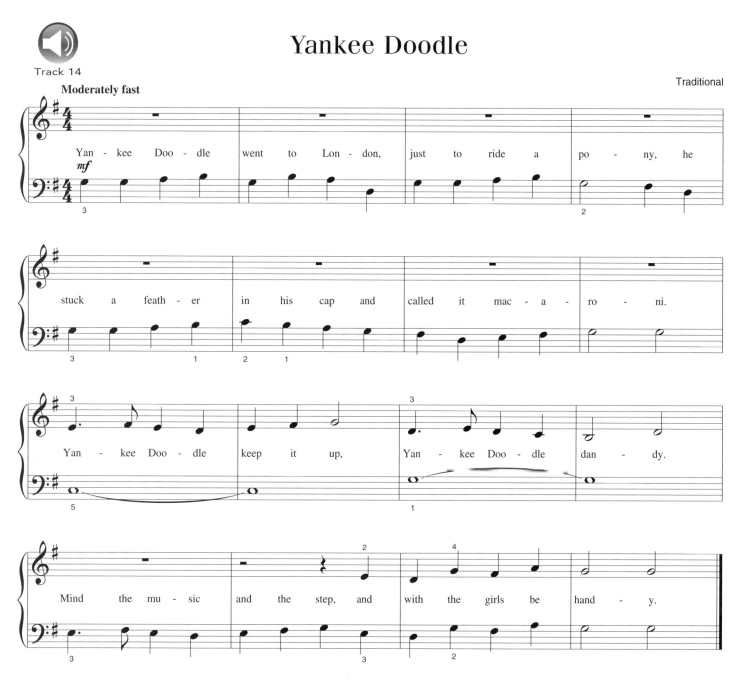

Key Signature Review

Sharps or flats placed immediately to the right of the clef sign are called the **key signature**, and determine the key, or tonal center of the song. Those sharps or flats named in the key signature are altered for the entire song.

Strategies for Playing Hands Together

When learning to play songs notated on the grand staff, it sometimes helps to study each staff separately. If you're unsure about bass staff notes, this is the time to really review and learn the left-hand part. Sometimes it's the right-hand part that could be challenging, especially if there are many hand-position shifts or fingering changes. When in doubt, it's always a good idea to practice each hand alone. Let's look at some specific examples.

Strategies

"Bravery" is a classical piece by 18th century composer Daniel Gottlob Türk. There are fewer notes to play in the left hand, so let's start with the bass staff.

Beginning with left-hand thumb on middle C, you will not have to move your hand until the very last measure, when you stretch your 5th finger down to reach the low C. Play the bass staff part with your left hand now, being sure to hold each whole note for four counts.

Before you play the right-hand part, glance through the measures looking for any moves or shifts. In this case, right hand stays in one place for the entire piece. Play the right-hand part alone until you've learned the melody securely.

Play both hands together. Before you begin, choose a tempo that will allow you to play easily and without pausing or stopping. Are there places you need to go back to review? Try hands together again or isolate a spot that might be difficult or confusing. "Bravery" is marked "Moderato." Can you play this piece easily at a moderate tempo?

Bravery

By Daniel Gottlob Türk

Track 15

"America," sometimes known as "My Country, 'Tis of Thee," has a well-known melody played by the right hand. Review the melody, noting the hand shifts and fingering changes. Play the left-hand part alone. How many different notes are in the bass staff? Play hands together slowly at first. You may wish to sing as you play to help propel you along.

America

Words by Samuel Francis Smith
Music from *Thesaurus Musicus*

Track 16

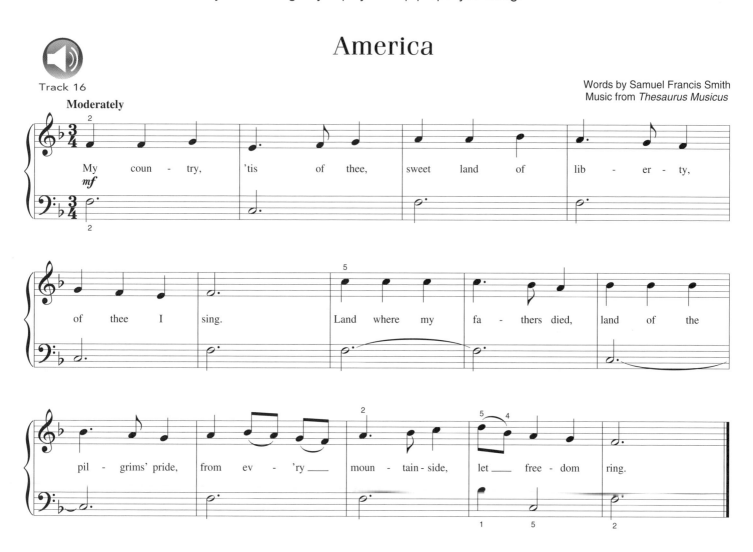

More Strategies

Don't be intimidated by left-hand parts that contain more than one note at a time. Usually these are easier to read than you think. Analyze the intervals and look for notes that stay the same from one interval (or measure) to the next. Let's take a look at the bass staff of "Largo from Symphony No. 9 ("New World")." Play these first eight measures, taking note of the intervals marked.

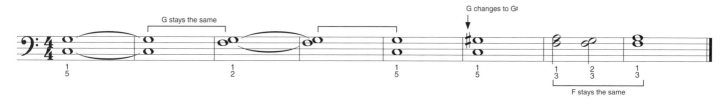

The next eight measures contain only two different thirds that alternate.

Largo from Symphony No. 9
("New World")

By Antonin Dvořák

Left-Hand Accompaniment Patterns

Lesson 6

You may be starting to notice that often the left hand is quite patterned. Learning to recognize common accompaniment patterns can make reading the bass staff easier.

Chords

You've had some experience with chordal accompaniment already, in "Largo from Symphony No. 9 ("New World")." Chordal accompaniments can be quite static or move around greatly. The chords themselves can change at a slow rate or quickly. In the example below, left hand plays just four chords, moving down a key each time. Each chord gets two beats in the first two measures, and then the chords double in speed when they change to quarter notes.

Track 18

Arpeggios

Arpeggios (broken chords) are also a frequent accompaniment pattern. Remember, "broken" chords are full chords played one note at a time instead of all together.

Track 19

Independent Lines

Sometimes the left-hand part is entirely independent of the right-hand part. It may be melodic, or fully harmonic, and more complex than a blocked or broken chord.

Sight-read the bass staff measures below. Note the fingering. When learning a piece with entirely independent lines, both lines must be secure before playing them together.

Track 20

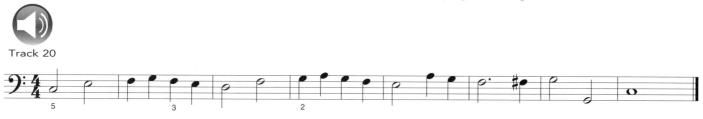

Putting It Together

Chordal Accompaniment

Playing blocked chords is an easy way to give a full sound to a simple melody on the piano. Add the chord pattern you just practiced in lesson 6 to "The Cat Came Back."

The Cat Came Back

Track 21

Words and Music by Harry S. Miller

Arpeggiated Accompaniment

"Du, Du Liegst Mir Im Herzen (You, You Weigh on My Heart)" is a lovely German folk song with an arpeggiated (broken chord) accompaniment. Notice that for most of the song, you are only playing two chords in the left hand, C and G7. The G7 chord has B as the root (or lowest) note of the chord. Look ahead to the last eight measures. Here the broken chords change to blocked chords for contrast.

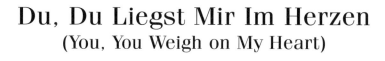

Du, Du Liegst Mir Im Herzen
(You, You Weigh on My Heart)

German Folksong

Track 22

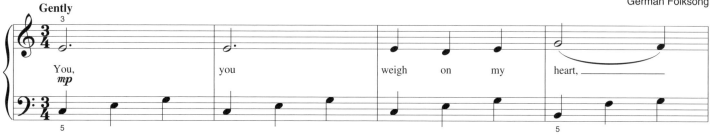

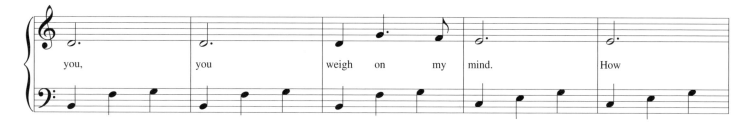

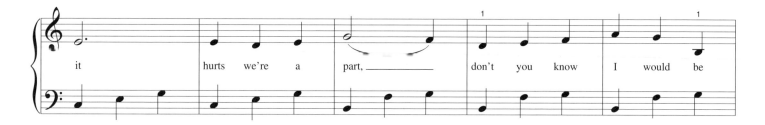

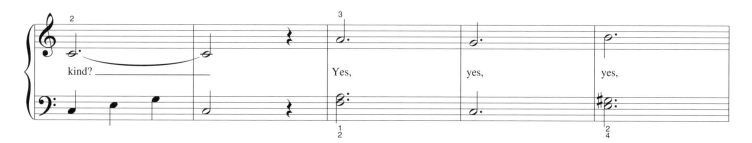

Independent Lines

"Little Invention" is short but complex. Both hands play melodic lines that intertwine. Learn each hand carefully before playing hands together. Challenge yourself! Sing one line while playing the other line.

Little Invention

By Jakub Jan Ryba

Track 23

The left hand echoes the right hand for the first four measures of "A Conversation." Here again, you'll want to learn each hand alone before playing hands together. After taking the repeat under the first ending bracket, skip those first ending measures to take the second ending.

A Conversation

By Béla Bartók

Track 24

Bass Lines and the Blues

Groovy bass lines are one of the most fun things to play with left hand. Whether it's a repeated chord pattern, "walking" bass, or just a jazzy little riff, these are places the left hand can really shine.

The left-hand part in "Hesitation Blues" is quite simple. There are two places where the left hand adds some interest. In measures 5-6 the eighth-dotted-quarter rhythm echoes the right hand and pushes the beat along.

Under the first and second ending brackets the left hand has a little riff to play. Practice moving from the B♭ to B♮.

Hesitation Blues

Track 25

Words and Music by Billy Smythe
and J. Scott Middleton

Moderately

The left-hand part in "Freight Train" is so much fun to play! Take a look at the opening measures.

The D chord is outlined, with a bit of a "walk" up the scale in measure 2. The A chord is outlined starting in measure 5, and the F#7 chord in measures 11-12. Practice playing each of these patterns with your left hand on its own before you play the whole song.

Freight Train

Words and Music by
Elizabeth Cotten

The driving left-hand 5ths and 6ths give "Worried Man Blues" its old-timey character. Use fingers 2 and 5 to play the fifth so you can switch to fingers 1 and 5 on the sixth. Don't be afraid to lean into the eighth note whenever the eighth-dotted-quarter note rhythm occurs. Take your time with this lazy blues and let the lyrics tell the story.

Worried Man Blues

Track 27

Traditional

Coordination and Syncopation

The ability to move smoothly from one hand to the other or play different notes and rhythms in each hand at the same time is crucial as you advance to more difficult music. Here are a few simple exercises to strengthen both your fingers and coordination skills.

Five-Note Scale Exercises

As the five-note scale moves from left hand to right hand, make sure the tempo flows smoothly without a pause. Choose a slow tempo first, and gradually increase to a faster tempo.

Track 28

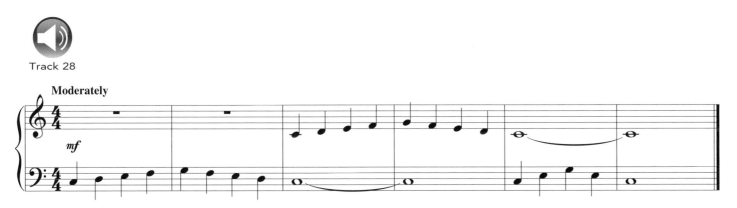

This next exercise is a bit trickier. If you play each hand separately, you'll see that both play a simple 5-note scale. Play as slowly as necessary to keep the tempo steady, without stopping or pausing.

Track 29

Both of these exercises can be played with variations:

- Right hand staccato, left hand legato
- Left hand staccato, right hand legato
- Right hand forte, left hand piano
- Left hand forte, right hand piano

"Für Elise" is one of Beethoven's most famous keyboard pieces. One of the challenges when performing this piece is to smoothly connect the notes in a singing manner, and also to smoothly connect the notes as they move between the hands. The arrangement below is abridged and simplified, but still allows you to practice these important techniques while enjoying this classic melody.

Track 30

Für Elise

By Ludwig van Beethoven

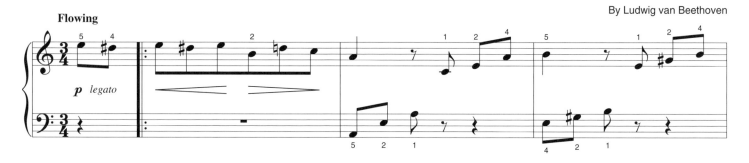

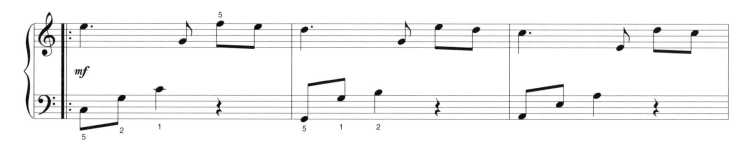

Practice tips for Für Elise

1. Notice the left-hand patterns. In measures 2-9 there are two alternating measures in the left hand. Measures 10-11 are different. Practice the left-hand part alone.

2. Work with the hairpin *crescendo* and *decrescendo* to help shape the right-hand phrase. Listen for a smooth, connected sound that rises and falls.

3. Playing hands together, think ahead as each hand "trades off" within the measure.

4. In measures 13-15, keep counting eighth notes as you alternate E in each hand.

5. Play this piece at a slow tempo until all notes and rhythms are secure and easy to play.

Syncopation

Syncopation occurs when weak beats are accented. A very common syncopation is the eighth-quarter-eighth rhythm found in the arrangement of "He's Got the Whole World in His Hands" on the next page. Right hand plays the syncopated melody against a steady rhythm in left hand. Knowing each part securely is necessary to perform this song confidently.

Singing along will help you get comfortable with the melody. Challenge yourself to count aloud, subdividing the right-hand part in eighth notes: "one-and-two-and-three-and-four-and" for even more security.

In the second half of the arrangement, left hand switches to a fun walking bass line. Practice this alone at first, looking out for accidentals and fingering shifts. If playing hands together here is challenging, try tapping the rhythm hands together as you count aloud, lining up the eighth notes against the steady quarter notes. Slow down the tempo as needed.

He's Got the Whole World in His Hands

Traditional Spiritual

Highlighting the Left Hand

In this simplified version of "Moonlight" Sonata Theme, both hands play a continuous broken-chord pattern. Right hand introduces the pattern, and then switches to melody in measure 10. At measure 11 left hand plays broken chords supporting the right-hand melody. The chords change frequently but moves are minimal.

"Moonlight" Sonata Theme

Track 32

By Ludwig van Beethoven

Adagio

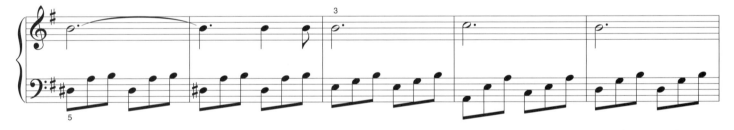

Notice the (♫ = ♩♪) after the tempo head designating swing eighths in "Midnight Special." This creates an eighth-note feel of "long-short" adding to the bluesy character of this classic. Identify the chord changes and practice moving from chord to chord as the harmony shifts in the left hand before adding the right hand. Once you know where you're going, relax and let the left hand drive this tune.

Midnight Special

Track 33

Railroad Song

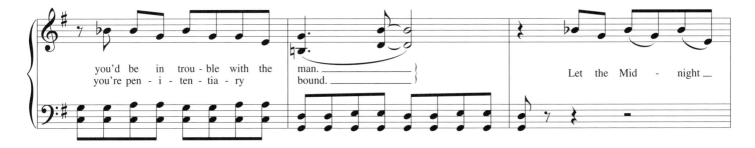

you'd be in trou - ble with the
you're pen - i - ten - tia - ry

man.
bound.

Let the Mid - night

Spe - cial

shine her light on

me.

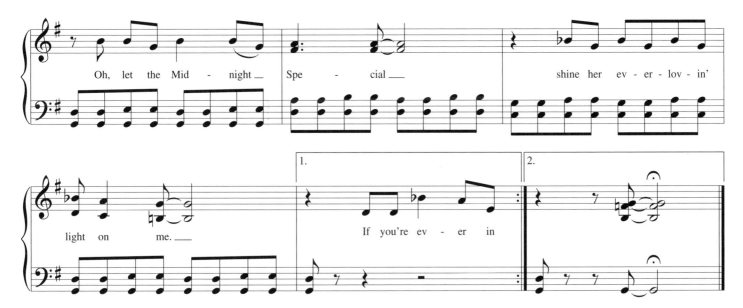

Oh, let the Mid - night Spe - cial

shine her ev - er - lov - in'

light on me.

1.

If you're ev - er in

2.

The traditional Scottish "Skye Boat Song" beginning on p. 30 exemplifies how much impact strong left-hand writing can have. While the left hand never plays the melody, it supports the right hand with flowing accompaniment, provides rhythmic interest with a syncopated section, and finally, leaves the listener with a feeling a peace and strength through the use of blocked intervals. Divide this arrangement into sections as you learn each accompaniment style, first with left hand, adding right hand when left hand is secure.

Skye Boat Song

Traditional Scottish

Flowing along

mp

poco rit.

With pedal

mf a tempo

mf

f

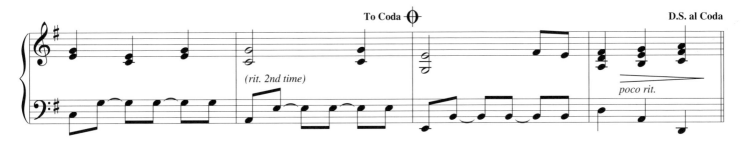

To Coda ⊕   D.S. al Coda

(rit. 2nd time)

poco rit.

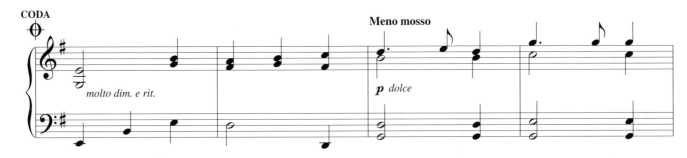

CODA ⊕   Meno mosso

molto dim. e rit.   *p* dolce

ten.

ten.

molto rit. al fine   *pp*

8vb

Left hand plays melody in "Night Escape." Use the long slurs to help identify and shape each phrase. Practicing one phrase at a time is an excellent way to learn this piece carefully. First play the melody, using the fingering given and listening for a smooth, legato sound. Study the right-hand chords. There are seven different chords to play; always seconds or thirds with minimal movement. Work through the slight shifts and changes in each phrase of the right-hand part, playing hands together only after each hand is well understood and comfortable. Practice at a super slow tempo at first. When you can play confidently at a slow tempo it will be easy to increase the tempo. As you work on each phrase, also note the dynamics.

Night Escape

Track 35

By Cornelius Gurlitt